TAKING A DETOUR:

ADAPTING THEATRE TO CELEBRATE THE ABILITY OF ALL

SAM WITH KATHY HOTCHNER

This book is dedicated to every
actor whose dream is to be on stage

Although the Detour journey adapts theatre for the non-
traditional actor, the destination is the same:

Telling a compelling story

Committing to artistry

Engaging the audience

We want to thank The Molly Lawson Foundation and Bobbie Davis
for their generous support of this project

Table of Contents

Listen With Your Heart

People often ask me why I began Detour. I'm over-the-top passionate about theatre, accessibility and opportunity, but the underlying reason was because my son asked. In that one sincere question something in my heart heard not only his voice but the voices of his friends, my students and all who deserved and longed for their chance to be on stage.

At the time this "detour" absolutely re-navigated my own personal journey, I was teaching theatre at Phoenix Day School for the Deaf. My son Christopher, who was multi-brain damaged at birth, would often meet me at the school after his workday at a nearby sheltered work shop. He would trudge in, eagerly get my keys and come to life as he "did his thing" on the stage across the hall from my classroom. Together we'd play all the games I was using for my students. Late one afternoon after locking up the stage Christopher turned to me and simply asked, "So, when's it going to be my turn?" I said, "What do you mean? You get to do theater all the time." "No," He shook his head. "When's it going to be my turn to be IN a show?" I had to pause and really consider what he was asking. The pure honesty of that very valid question lodged in my brain and took hold of my heart. I spent the rest of that year trying to find a theater program that was more than recreational games, more than therapy, that offered a process centered approach to creating authentic theatre (REAL shows). I wanted to find a theater organization that would teach acting skills, emphasize theater responsibility and encourage possibility but not stop there. I wanted lights, costumes, scripts, music, choreography and standing ovations. When I couldn't find that program I talked to the man I loved most in the world and he offered me three words. "Start one yourself." I took a leave of absence from my job and never looked back.

We started with a handful of starry-eyed actors. A few years later, when we had 24 actors, I said we hit our limit. Then our limit was 30, then 40, then 50. The challenge then, as it is now, was that I'd get phone calls from parents eager for their sons and daughters to have this chance. I've never advertised for actors, never. But people hear about us. They see a production or someone is a friend of someone who is in Detour. Parents would (and still do) call me with stories about how their sons and daughters have been singing and dancing in the living room for years and how they want a chance to do it on a real stage, under real lights. I can't be one more person to tell these parents, and even worse their children, "no." I can't even say, "can your child memorize? Can your child speak and enunciate in a way that can be understood? Can your child move?" Now, after more than 18 years we have had up to 52 actors and 23 coaches on stage (though I do believe that it is best to really limit a show to 45 actors tops). I use a live band and we have a musical director with us weekly. We use three American Sign Language interpreters for each show—two for the audience, one for deaf actors on stage. We have someone who provides audio-describing for our audience members who are blind and a coach who provides audio-description for those actors who also need this service. Now new hopefuls wanting to be in Detour join our "Boots Camp" program—a place to learn about theater and perform small sections of musicals. We run a summer program and have launched a traveling troupe.

Detour clearly is not about recreational games, though we do play lots of games. Detour is not about therapy though, without question, creating theater has always had a powerful therapeutic effect. Detour is not about the product, though we are always incredibly proud of the shows we produce. Detour is an authentic theater company for the many adults who daily live with life challenges including, but not limited to, Autism, Blindness, Down Syndrome, Deafness, Cerebral Palsy and so many other "quirky" conditions that fall "in between."

Detour is about Yes! It offers both opportunity and possibility for a group of all too often marginalized adults in our society. For the vast majority of this population, once they turn 22, they age out of a system that has given them support and multiple things to do. What's left is to bag groceries, clean remotes and live in group homes with very little creative expression in their days and little to look forward to beyond Special Olympics and monthly dances. Detour offers an alternative. It's a place to shine, to become more, to embrace new skills, to inhabit someone else's skin and experience life and a myriad of different endings. What we strive to do is to take a journey that leads off the expected path. I simply teach what I love. We "try on life." I do Detour because this group of people should be recognized and celebrated for the wondrous gifts they offer.

I was driving through road construction mulling over what I could call this company of folks when all of a sudden I encountered a blinking sign telling me to detour. That was it. When we take a detour we take a different kind of journey. Detours usually force us to slow down and they always offer the chance to see something we may not have noticed otherwise. That's the attitude we strive to carry into our work. We get there. We do it our way. That "detour journey" is what we are honored to share here.

CHAPTER 1

Detour Pedagogy

My MFA degree is in theater and my first love is dance. Together these two have always informed my work with Detour. We follow a pedagogy of learning, using tried and true theatre games that are adapted to have meaning for our actors. These theatre skills are taught progressively. Games can be used in any number of ways, to emphasize any number and combination of skills. What's so vitally important is to always tell the group the "why" and "what" of each particular activity. "Why" is it important we play this game or do this activity now and in this order. "What" did they learn from the interaction. It's never a secret that the skills being taught in rehearsal are exactly the ones to be applied when blocking a scene later (whether it be later that day or weeks in the future.) You must know the answers to "Why" and "What" to all you do—each precious moment. Trust that knowledge. When you, as teacher and director, truly understand this process, everything else comes together.

We use five stages of game/activity development that move us from game to stage. What follows is a list of games. A more detailed explanation of many of these games is included in chapter 4.

Awareness

This is the first step on the journey. One must experience and feel confident with this before moving on to do anything else. Awareness of self . . . . Who am I? How do I move? What can my body do? How much space do I take up? How do I control, express, or choose not to express my own emotions.

Activities and vocabulary that explore self-awareness:

Levels—high medium low
Freeze / Make a Shape

Slow motion/ Fast motion
Walks—in different environments, as characters, as creatures, etc.

Simple blocking vocabulary—(cheat out and stage directions)

When you are aware of yourself, you can begin to take on the characteristics of a given role and become aware of who that character is and what makes him, her or it the same and/or different from you.

When you are truly aware of yourself, you can begin to honor and become aware of others…which leads to focus.

Focus

After we become aware of ourselves, we are invited to become aware of others. Focus is the natural next step. Giving focus is one of the most important things we do with others both in our everyday lives and on stage. Giving focus indicates that we are paying attention. It helps us know how and when to respond and it lets others (especially on stage) know exactly what or who they should be watching. Giving focus is always the first step in "seeing" others.

Activities and vocabulary that explore focus

Heartbeat (ball pass in circle)
1,2,3, focus
Mirror game with a partner
Mirror game as a group
Match me
1,2,3 change
Bean bag toss—with bean bag
Imaginary Ball toss (Matching size and weight of ball)
ball toss with multiple balls
change the object
All kinds of pantomime activities

Relationships (Character)

After we are able to give focus to one another, we can begin to explore the fun of creating relationships with each other. Playing with relationships is the beginning of developing improvisational skills. It's the beginning of creating a story. An actor must maintain awareness and focus ESPECIALLY when interacting with another character. In exploring relationships and improvisation the most important word, we use, is "yes." Go with the information given and see where it leads.

Activities and vocabulary that explore relationships

Any and all open scenes
Simple dialogue from a given show—or let them suggest characters and create their own dialogue.
Build and break with a specific tableau
Character walks

Yes, No game with a partner
Open sentence (You did what to my car?)
Chair game (first person sits establishes the place, 2nd person establishes the relationship)

Reacting

Reacting leads to creating characters and relationships that are believable and stories that are understandable. The magic of watching a live stage production is in experiencing the ever changing reactions shared. "Acting IS reacting." These words, first taught to us by director David Helmstetter, have become our mantra. Our "reactions" are what make theatre real, worth watching and, ultimately bring a story to life.

Everything done so far can be done adding or emphasizing a given emotion, and/or an attitude.

using emotions with:
walks

shapes
as part of 1,2,3 change
with build and break
blocking (This is what makes blocking come alive … what do they think the playwright wants conveyed)

Story

We could go back and forth between awareness, focus, relationships and reacting and create theatre classes full of meaning—enough to last a life time. But Detour is about more. It is all about this 5th element. It is all about taking those first four elements and weaving them together to bring a story to life on stage. We then add lights, music, choreography, costumes, sets and so forth. We add it all knowing it all goes back to support awareness, sharing focus, knowing who we are in relationship to the others who share that specific environment, and reacting to what is happening about us. We rehearse our story again and again. Everything is thrown into the mix and somehow directors, musical directors, coaches,

actors all get it. Story is the heart beat of what we do. In our very first game we urge our actors not to drop that bean bag. We pass it around in a circle. We stress the importance of keeping the story going no matter what.

Creating a fabulous story is why we are all ultimately there. For many reasons, and each in our way, we show up to respond to that invitation to "try on life." It's that process that changes us forever.

CHAPTER 2

About Scripts

Choosing a show and introducing its story are vital aspects of script work. There are many factors that go into choosing a show. One of the first is to discover what is the show's theme and its relevance to my actors. Next, I have to consider whether it is a story they know, easier, or one they will be excited and challenged to learn, harder, but an important opportunity to honor. I always look at content. It can't be too adult nor can it be too childish. It must be engaging for the actors and the audience. I must consider the characters—how many men, women, chorus members, etc. Finally, can this story live through a bit of tweaking and will the relevance still shine through?

I always identify a theme within a script. As director it's the first thing I do and it's what I stress with my actors. Our themes vary, but they always have something to do with who we are in Detour. For *Beauty and the Beast*, the theme wasn't finding beauty, rather sharing kindness. It is an act of kindness when Belle offers to take her father's place in the castle. Perhaps it is because the Beast has witnessed this kindness that he, in turn, protects Belle from the wolves. Our actors were encouraged to find those pivotal moments when sharing an act of kindness made the difference.

It gave the story far more meaning. We refer back to that theme at the close of every rehearsal—have we honored it? It's a challenge sometimes but there is always a theme. Our theme for Shrek was acceptance of someone who is different, for *Adams Family* it was the loyalty of family. I'm a teacher. As much as the goal of theatre is to entertain, I feel this process and our final product must also teach.

Even before we begin auditions and casting, I must know the script and have an idea of how our huge family of actors can fit the roles needed. Adjusting text to fit this company is a sacred and huge challenge. I want to give every actor a special moment to shine. I want to give everyone who can speak, even minimally, at least one line. The challenge is finding and creating enough spoken opportunities within the story. As our company has grown, we have tried many different approaches. We found that double casting lead roles helps, as does dividing a single character between a group of actors. Sometimes there are more meaningful ways to involve what would ordinarily be a chorus member.

When Detour began I used the scripts of Alan Prewit who was a local playwright. All through our early years he let me make changes in order to "Detourize" his work. I learned about actors sharing a role, I learned how to adapt lines and I learned the magic of tweaking a script to make it fit our group. As we grew we began leasing popular Broadway shows and paying royalties. This has meant there are far more rules to abide by. I still must "Detourize" to some extent. Before I even lease a show I make sure that publishers know we must have permission to Braille a script, that our show will be interpreted for the Deaf and that my actors have other challenges that may impact our unique production.

So what does it mean, to "Detourize" a script? How do we create shared roles which allow us to give opportunity to multiple actors with very different abilities? For example, in our production of *Mary Poppins*, we couldn't fly any actors. Instead we chose to fly in Mary's parasol. The actor who "caught" the parasol as it was lowered became part of a Mary Poppins trio we created. I cast an actor with a beautiful voice to play Mary Poppins. She is also blind which meant she needed a sighted guide. We then named the guide actor Molly Poppins. She was given the lines that came from visual cues. Our Mary was able to do the singing and the majority of dialogue. The actor who caught the flying parasol we named Polly Poppins. She has minimal speech but she was able to say "spit spot" and point the parasol in the direction they were all to exit. She had her moment to shine and was an active part of the Mary Poppins trio.

In our production of *Fiddler on the Roof* I didn't want to lose any of Yenta's lines, which are many. We split the full Yenta role, without changing a word, between four wonderful actors who practiced speaking quickly and interrupting one another, in order to create a sisterhood of Yentas.

The magic of Detour is finding the "off the beaten track" solution to how we can make every person feel like he or she is an integral piece of making every performance happen.

CHAPTER 3

Being the Director

Over the years I've learned side by side with my actors. I give my-self to the work, to the story, to each show with the same energy, commitment and belief I ask of them. Together we've figured out what works and what isn't quite as successful. It can be hard to "let go" of some of what is traditionally taught as the "director approach" but Detour is its own unique journey that results in ac-tive, emotional and thoughtful responses. I never sit down behind a table with the script spread out in front of me. I don't sit. I need to be up among the actors, showing them how I want them to move, where I want them go.

We do learn stage directions but often it's easier to reference the kitchen of our rehearsal space (SL) or the parking lot (SR.) Because skill levels differ greatly from actor to actor, I often mirror blocking as I negotiate where I'd like my actors to be and what I'd like them to do. Ours is a very hands on process. Even those actors who aren't as comfortable being touched become used to me being near, hugging them (by permission only,) and often helping them move from one place to another. I come to each and every practice with blocking prepared—that's my homework—but, more often than not, I am always aware that I may need to throw it all out—that's my reality.

For many of my actors, everything a script says is taken quite literally. We invest a lot of necessary time talking through each character's blocking. When we did *Footloose*, I cast a group of "not as experienced" boys as the "bullies". No one wanted to be in that group when they found out they had to beat up Ren. Their hesitant attitudes became a problem for me. As a director I spend a lot of time unraveling what looks like indifference, or resistance until I figure out the real problem. In that situation, I discovered my boys couldn't separate the fantasy of the story (bullies beating up Ren) from their own personal behavioral plans (PBP) that state there can be no anger or aggression without consequences. I had to patiently explain that this was to be their actor challenge—it became a critical teaching moment. My job was to help them become the most convincing "bully" possible. We changed everything making every movement much larger than life and then manipulated the speed so the big "fight" was a slow motion dance of sorts—with absolutely no physical contact. That little tweak helped them achieve success. These are the kinds of discoveries that are most important for me as a director.

For many of my actors, it's a problem when a script calls for two characters to kiss. As one wondrous young actor with Autism told me, "I just don't do that kind of intimacy." It takes extra time and carefully orchestrated rehearsals with just the two actors involved to figure out how to navigate this hurdle. Sometimes the reason is that the actors involved are shy and too embarrassed to kiss. Sometimes it's a concern because they're "kissing" another actor's sweet heart. Sometimes it's simply because they're afraid to show affection in front of others. Many with Autism just don't like the physical contact. We adapt. We kiss hands. We come close to kissing. We build excitement and then let the moment be interrupted. We blow a kiss or hold a lingering look. Again, that's the challenge—and the joy—of directing. The ideas for solving a problem follow quite logically once you figure out the stumbling block. When we performed *Happy Days,* our Fonzie and Pinky (their stage character names) were both in relationships with other actors. "Pinky" was especially concerned that her boyfriend, cast as one of the high school boys, would be upset when the Fonz kissed her.

We talked about it at length. While it was true that our actress, as herself, wouldn't kiss the actor playing the Fonze, it was absolutely true that Pinky WOULD. We established a goal together. Our actress' personal challenge was to NOT be herself in the play, she was to become totally Pinky and of course, Pinky just couldn't wait for that kiss. We began working that scene by first looking into one another's eyes, next we progressed to holding hands. Once they were comfortable with that, the actor playing the Fonze kissed Pinky's hand as she held it just in front of her lips. Slowly we worked on developing the trust and confidence necessary to have Pinky lower her hand. Finally, they were both invested in their roles enough to allow that magical moment to happen. They shared a kiss, the moment was real, and the audience cheered.

My job as director is to be a detective. I'm always working to "look deeper" as I watch the interaction on stage. I must see beyond what my actors are doing. I look for what else could be happening in the story, where I might add a moment or tweak. In *Hairspray* we had the whole chorus stop singing and freeze during the final refrain of one song. An actress with very minimal speech had the line, "Go Mama go." It was to be delivered as she handed off a boa to Edna. It required more than a few seconds for this dear actor to muster all she had in order to get those words out. We all understood that. It didn't matter. We waited, we focused. That's another essential directing lesson.

If your actors are focused on something, the audience realizes you are engaged in what's happening and amazingly enough the audience will wait patiently with you. For that show, the music stopped, the actors stopped. The audience watched. We waited and we waited a little bit more. It didn't matter. It was her moment. When the words spilled out the audience cheered and we took a breath and moved on. She held the moment in her heart. We could all see that as she beamed with satisfaction.

There are three things my actors hear me say over and over again. These are the important truths I teach about directing. The first is "FOCUS." Look at one another and be aware of what you are communicating to the audience. Many of my actors can learn their lines, even invest them with emotion, but getting them to focus as they are speaking them can be a much harder leap. Turning their backs to the audience to face someone they are talking to is a natural movement and coaches are constantly turning their actors around. The 2nd truth is "BE OFF BOOK." It can't be stated enough. As the director that deadline is vital for you to set. The quicker you get scripts out of your actors hands the quicker you can put props in. Only when books are off stage can faces finally look up and hands be opened to respond. Which leads to the third truth "REACT." As a director my job is to coax every reaction I can out of my actors. It is what they want to do and what the audience is there to celebrate. This reacting is what keeps us engaged in the story. All of that tweaking, exploring, trying again and again and again is what makes directing Detour a challenge, a tremendous investment of time and totally worth every magical moment.

My coaches would add a fourth directing truth and it's probably what would be inscribed on my headstone. . . .write in pencil and bring an eraser. Everything can and probably will change.

CHAPTER 4

Early Rehearsal Process

A Detour production session is approximately four months long (September through December for our early January show. February—May for our early June show.) Weekly, during this time, every Thursday, our goal is to give each and every actor an authentic experience of learning, growing and creating theatre through a "process" centered approach that explores theatre from the inside out. It's all quite magical—it's all about each actor truly experiencing success and pride in his or her work. The show may be the ultimate, long range product but weekly we provide a chance to share, evaluate, reflect upon and celebrate the variety of skills learned. Implicit in this approach is great community building, ample opportunities to demonstrate responsible choices, observation, participation, enhance social skills (listening, speaking, responding) and finally all the singing, dancing, blocking and dialogue every theatre company offers.

The whole family of Detour meets together EVERY Thursday. Right now that means close to 50 actors, working side by side with 20 or more coaches. Thursday is the day we typically set aside to do all the large group choreography, all the full group songs, all the crossovers, the finale, bows—everything that requires we have everybody on stage. It's massive, chaotic and very exciting.

Mondays and Fridays I meet with smaller groups. And, just because I can't say no, and because it's really necessary for many individuals, I work Wednesdays and many weekends with single actors or duos. It's a lot of work but it's an investment in heartfelt dreams.

Our practice room is set up with as huge a circle of chairs as we can manage—a piano facing all. This open work space is non-negotiable. It is important that we be able to actually see each other while we talk with one another.

Introductions & getting to know each other

A game we use with new actors or at the start of a session is "favorites." The leader asks the group, "What's your favorite _____?" (movie, pet, drink etc.) As each person says her/his favorite _____, all the others in the circle who also like that same food (sport, movie, fast food etc.) stand up. It's a quick way to access shared likes or dislikes. The final question for an activity such as this is, "So, what did you notice? What surprised you?"

An alternate take on "Favorites" is to have them stand as the leader goes through a list. "Stand if you like pizza. Stand if you work in a work shop setting. Stand if you have on jeans today." They can be crazy or serious statements—either way the job of the group is to notice the others who are standing when they are. You can end by telling them, " Say hello to another actor who likes dogs" or "greet an actor who likes the same movies you do." Observation is important. This is an easy first introduction to mastering that skill.

Often actors walk in our door immediately after they've finished a long or troubling day. There are many theatre exercises for dealing with that. What follows is one I like to use. I tell the group:

> Think about everything that has happened to you today up to your walking into this room—in just a minute you're going to put some of "that stuff" in a pile on the floor in front of you. You can include anything you'd like to get rid of—going to work this morning, being stuck in traffic, spilling your coffee, anything that happened—anything you don't want to carry around. Next, as you imagine whatever that negative, sad or angry thing was, place it into your hand. Close your hand tightly. Shake it. Carefully place that experience on the floor in front of you. Repeat this process for everything you want to get rid of. Finally, take your foot and really squish that pile down. Step on it. Harder. Get rid of it. Step on it again and push it under your seat and behind you. For the next two hours all of that stuff is gone. Really gone. Out of sight. Now, be here. Open your hands—be ready to pick up something new, something better.

A "Survival" Technique

Home Base is not a game but we have learned to play it like one.

Early on in the directing process, I assign everyone a specific place where they sit or stand as part of our full company. It may or may not be related to the beginning of the show or the finale. It's a place every actor knows to go to anytime I say home base. That way I can see who is missing. When things get chaotic I find that everyone needs a home base position where they can be counted and then be counted upon.

The Importance of Games

Games are central to what and how we teach. Every game can be used to emphasize and further a multitude of different skills. What's important to be aware of is, for that specific day, that specific lesson, what is the "take away" you hope to achieve. Without thinking this part through games become time fillers. With this knowledge and the knowledge of how to adapt and change games, they become a central component for establishing a vital and relevant pedagogy.

When I talk about pedagogy I am talking about the sequence of learning. Each session builds from past lessons—on a larger scale even the rehearsal process reflects this purposeful scaffolding. Over the years we've come up with a sequence of skill building that works for us. This is a brief retelling of Chapter 1. We begin with AWARENESS—of ourselves first. Once we are fully aware of ourselves, we become aware of others. That is is what we call FOCUS. Once we are comfortable with that we move on to RELATIONSHIP. This is key for beginning improvisation and characterization. From there REACTING flows naturally. All four come together to create meaningful STORY, our fifth component. Sometimes story is a single afternoon activity or sometimes it is months of exploring a script. In every way—for it to be successfully understood—it is the culmination of how we weave together awareness, focus, relationships and reacting.

I begin our early sessions with games and activities that we refer back to again and again during the rehearsal process. It's never a secret that the skills being taught in rehearsal are exactly the ones to be applied later when blocking a scene. Many of these activities are from familiar theatre and/or game books. Like every other teacher we bend and shape them. We take "detours" to make them fit. I try to figure out how to make them work for those who are blind, or deaf, or have minimal movement. We discover together.

Heart Beat

I hold up a ball, a bean bag, something that can be easily identified and easily passed. I start passing it around as I explain, "this is the heart beat. It represents the story. No matter what, even as I am talking about random stuff, you must keep the heartbeat going. No matter what, it is your job as actors to keep the story going. What happens if your heart beat stops? That's right, you're dead. So if the story stops, it's dead. Especially on stage, it's all about the story."

At this point I begin passing other random objects, balls, bean bags, even props from the show. Sometimes I pass in the same direction as the designated heart beat sometimes in the opposite direction. No matter what object they are passed, the goal is to keep the heart beat object going—safely, successfully.

Here's how passing the heart beat relates to performance. If you forget a line what are you supposed to do? Keep the show going! Don't let the story die. The audience doesn't have a script.

Shape 1-2-3

With Shape 1-2-3 we first begin by creating individual shapes. (AWARENSS) Sometimes you must break activities down to their most basic terms. You must explain what it means to be neutral and then what it means to change the body and freeze—(or hold that position.) That is creating a shape. We begin with abstract shapes.

After creating shapes we add levels. This is where things become fun, interesting, challenging and as unique as the group you are working with. Shapes can be high, low or medium. A very tall actor can still make a very low shape. A very short actor can stand very tall. It's fun to challenge them to see things that are obvious in new and creative ways.

Once everyone understands about levels, shapes and freezes we're ready to play. I put my actors in groups of three.

When I say, "go" they must immediately create one group shape of three actors working together. Each person must become one of the three levels. There is no planning or discussion. The fun is in the spontaneity. When I say change, each of the trio must choose a different level. No two actors in a group should be at the same level. We continue to change and freeze until the actors are comfortable with this process.

As always, we end with, "What things did you notice?" "What worked for you?" "What was hard? Why?"

After mastering this process, Shape 1-2-3 becomes very useful for choreography. For example, while learning the chorus of "Let Your Freak Flag Fly," from *Shrek* I just counted 1,2,3 and said "make a shape," and they got it. When I said, "change," they were able to change shapes and levels without a problem. If I had had to choreograph everyones' position, it would have taken forever and not been nearly as interesting. Actors love owning their own choreography.

Build & Break

Build and break naturally follows Shape 1-2-3. It is a game that introduces tableau. I thank teaching artists Patrick Ziglarski and Alison Marshall for sharing this game that's become central to Detour work.

First I teach my actors that they can connect with a person in three ways: focus, physical contact and /or proximity. This last one is often hard for them to master. It means you can be really close to a person—but you don't have to touch them—you're still connected to the tableau because you are standing close by. It's a great safety net for those with "touch" and/or eye contact issues.

With build and break you first make a group shape. (The build) Each person connects with at least one other person in one of the three ways explained. You have to be able to hold your shape and you must memorize where your individual shape is in relation to the others in the group.

Next I ask them to "break" or move away from the shape.

Finally, I say "build" and the goal is to quickly come together again to recreate an exact duplicate of the original group shape or tableau.

This game has become absolutely vital for blocking. We do all kinds of expanded learning with it. After they break, I ask them to build like they are walking through a variety of environments and with a variety of emotions. I ask them to both build and break in slow motion and/or fast motion.

All of this is used as we build tableaux (specific theatre pictures) rather than abstract group shapes. Sometimes we create our final stage picture first and come back to it again and again during the rehearsal process.

Rehearsal Closure

It's important to me and to the group that we end each rehearsal with some kind of closure that includes reflection. It can be as simple as the group singing one of the full cast songs from the show and then quickly discussing their feelings about it. Often I ask them to share what they've learned that day in max two words. This is a challenge, but with a large group it allows for far more participation. Sometimes there is only time to ask them to point to someone who has been outstanding (helpful, kind, etc.) during the afternoon's rehearsal. If we've totally run out of time I tell them I'll be waiting at the door. They have to tell me one thing they've learned before I'll let them leave. I really hold them to that. There has to be something they've gained from the precious time we've spent together.

CHAPTER 5

Telling the Play's Story

Before we begin auditions I tell the group the story of the play. I purposely use my coaches both to introduce them and because they model jumping in and trying on a new role. The more non-traditional this spontaneous casting is, the more fun it is, and the more the group pays attention. It's also important because even if some of the actors know the story, it's good for the full group to hear our "Detourized" version. I always have to emphasize that our show may (and most probably will) end up different from the movie version they may be more familiar with.

Though it is much harder, sometimes I choose shows that many are unfamiliar with. It's good for all to stretch by experiencing new and unchartered territory. This happened when we did *Fiddler on the Roof.* I told them we were doing *Fiddler* because it has a lot to do with family. Then I continued, "How many of you have turned on the news lately? How many of you have seen families fleeing their country? Today, as during the era of the pogroms of *Fiddler,* many families truly have no idea where they are going, only that they must leave their homeland through no fault of their own." We then did an exercise together in which everyone got up and we made a tight circle. I told them to hold hands, and to feel how wonderful it was to be connected as a family. I said "This is a community. Detour is your home, where you know everyone. But tomorrow you are going away. Remember the feel of this hand in your hand." Together we felt our way into the meaning of the last song of *Fiddler On the Roof.*

It is vital to encourage our actors to understand and "live" all the moments they are to share with their audience. I have to break down the story scene by scene for my actors. I cannot assume that will happen on their own. It doesn't. I usually do this during the small group or individual rehearsals. I find that many actors don't understand the lines, vocabulary, or nuances of language that they must memorize. I cannot assume that every actor goes home to a living situation where they can discuss the current play, its meaning and the actor's role. I often ask, "So what do these words mean?" During *Hairspray,* Edna and Wilbur share a touching and hilarious duet. One of the lines sung is, "You smell like limburger cheese." The actor, who sang these words, didn't understand the humor behind them. As soon as I explained that limburger smells like dirty socks but tastes delicious, both my actors got the joke. That line was delivered with absolute confidence and understanding.

CHAPTER 6

Auditions

In our mission statement we say we offer an authentic theater experience. If we are going to be authentic, we must hold auditions. I believe casting is the most important work a director does. With that thought in mind, I truly believe that the audition process should be fun, as well as a meaningful learning experience for all who participate. I use auditions as an opportunity to evaluate an actor's growth, be surprised by new accomplishments, and to celebrate all the effort they invest.

I always ask the group when we start, "Do we audition to be IN the play?" They all know the Detour answer, "No. We audition to see what role we get." Everyone participates. That's the challenge and the opportunity. Auditions don't have to be threatening. We audition everyday of our lives. We apply for jobs. We go into new social situations. We get introduced to new people. Every single one of these encounters is an audition. We are putting ourselves out there to be accepted, rejected or just evaluated to see where we "fit" or can best be used. In Detour, we teach that auditions aren't about rejection; auditions are about finding out where and how an actor fits into the life of a specific production.

I stress again and again that we don't audition to be in a show. We audition for a role. We audition to figure out how an actor has grown and, as with any other theatrical production, we audition to see what groupings of actors make sense.

I continually remind them that everyone on that stage is vitally important. In a Detour production everybody gets to participate. Somebody who has no lines can steal the show. When we did *The Music Man,* we had a young woman who, at every scene change, carried out a hat box. The boxes and the hats she pulled out grew progressively bigger until during the last three scene changes the audience finally caught on. They could hardly wait to watch her open each successive hat box and see what she would pull out next. The audience oooed and ahhed and, as the audience responded. she would primp and show off the latest rendition. That scene "stole the show." For many, it's still what they remember most about that production.

For me, a fun and challenging part of adapting every script is finding these magical moments. That search begins during auditions when I watch, really watch, what each actor can or can not do. I never change the feeling or intent of a character. I highly respect the copyright laws but I am aware of the phrase "reasonable accommodation" which helps me set the Detour bar for creating accessible character roles for actors with a variety of challenges.

As I begin the audition process, I explain that we are going to have everybody do the same thing. I tell them they're going to talk a little, sing a little, dance a little. Many of the coaches join me in taking notes but in the end casting is the director's job, period. Those decisions and that vision impacts the whole rehearsal process.

Auditions for speaking roles:

When we audition for speaking roles we often do it the traditional way, giving the actors scripts with short scenes to read. This works for the more verbal actors and for actors who can read. We encourage everyone to try out for any part they choose. It's wonderful to see some of the more courageous verbally challenged actors take a shot at reading for a larger role. When we do auditions I know we will be working with some actors who can't/ don't read but who can memorize lines. I continually stress that this is not a reading audition. We also will be working with actors who can read but can't retain many lines. We stress that we are not worrying about lengthy memorization.

Often we will do what we call an improvisation audition. We use scenes from the play we are getting ready to do and ask each group to perform a scene of their choice. For these there is no scripted dialogue. It's all improvised. Each actor is responsible for showing who their character is, what their relationship is to one another, where they are, and finally, most important, what the problem is. Surprises happen. Freed from text many actors do what they do best, which is simply act.

Example: Improvised scenes from our *Mary Poppins* auditions:

Scene 1. Michael & Jane don't want to go for a walk in the park but Mary and Bert do.

Scene 2. Winifred is giving a party and telling the cooks what to do. The cooks are clumsy and make lots of mistakes.

Scene 3. The family is waiting for the new Nanny to arrive when all of a sudden Miss Andrews, the holy terror, walks through the door.

When we audition I tell everyone that auditioning is really, really hard. Because of that we give all of our love and support to the people who are up there, being open and vulnerable. We treat them with respect. You don't get to say you're tired, you don't get to say you're bored, you don't get to say you've already seen that scene. You listen to the same lines as many times as it takes for everyone to have a chance—and you look to hear or see something that amazes you.

I believe that auditions are an opportunity for the actors to gain confidence. The process must not leave an actor questioning his or her worth. I praise the courage shown in each actor's audition because they put themselves out there. Their best is perfect for who they are as individuals. Show investment begins here with auditions. It continues as they all come together to become the community of that show. We're still competitive—there's no getting around it—but we do try to couch it in honest-to-goodness learning and respect.

Musical Auditions

We also hold group and solo singing auditions. We start the group singing auditions with everyone learning the same part of a song. It can be a verse, or a chorus—but I choose something from the show that we will be working on. For *Footloose*, we all sang "I Need a Hero" and "Footloose". We also teach the actors a few simple movements so we can see how well they can execute and learn the choreography.

Next, we put them into small groups and in that smaller grouping they audition the song for us. There is great safety in this. Many of our actors simply don't sing well. I'm looking for enthusiasm and gusto. At least they're up there and if all they get out is a note I notice.

The solo auditions are a more complex process. All the actors who want to audition for a solo part first sit around the piano and learn a short part of a song. We do "match me" with music much the way we do "match me" with shapes. When everyone is comfortable with the melody we separate the girls and boys, teaching each group a short part of a song from the show. After learning the song the groups are sent to another room or outside to practice. Finally, they return to the piano area and one by one they perform a solo audition. We often ask them to sing again taking on the characteristics of a given role—(an old man, a young girl, a pirate.)

CHAPTER 7

Casting

Detour casting is very different though it still holds elements in common with any typical casting. I don't deal only with who is more capable, who is a better dancer, who is this or that. We don't audition for a specific character in a show. We audition to be in the show. So, again, everybody gets to participate. You look at actors, you look at the fit, you look at the character they are to play, you look at all those things as you do in mainstream theater. You try to balance it all so it all makes sense. But, I also have to look at who takes public transportation, who rides with who, who is not allowed to work with another actor, whose parents and /or staff will support the learning of lines. That's the challenge.

I always tell parents and actors these simple rules. If this is your very first show you won't get many lines. We need to see what happens when the lights go out. We don't know what an actor is going to do in that first performance experience. We had an actor who was great through every rehearsal and when the lights went out opening night she wouldn't move onto the stage. We had always practiced with the work lights on and we didn't know she would be petrified of the dark. Now we always have blue lights on for scene changes and rarely do a full black out. We must also know if a new actor will listen to their coach through the actual show week. We have had to find actors who have disappeared in the bathrooms only to miss their entrances. After their second show, and with successive shows, the actors get more lines. If an actor has just had a principal role in a show, in most cases, they will have a different kind of role in the next show. We strive to give everyone a chance.

I make no bones about building up what you traditionally call more minor/support roles by giving them something that's really special to do. When a person has low language I sometimes create a role that gives them a chance to be out front. We have a young woman who is extremely challenged in both movement and speech. In *Shrek,* I gave her the job of dusting Farquad's crown. When I say everybody's role is important, it is. Dusting the crown was important because Farquad is obsessed with it.

Truly, one of the most important things we have to look at when casting is which parents will bring their actor to extra rehearsals. It really does matter. Transportation and parental support are vitally necessary, especially for larger roles. If it's the best person for a role but the parent won't be supportive or help their actor get to additional rehearsals I can't cast them. I can't use that person even though they deserve that opportunity; I can't do that to the rest of the company. When I cast the character of Tracy in *Hairspray* her parents were very excited. They drove constantly so that their daughter could rehearse again and again and again. That additional time helped her to learn her lines and take on that huge role. Her family was behind her all the way.

We have a few actors who ride bicycles to rehearsals. They are usually willing and able to practice any time scheduled. Uber and Lyft have made all the difference in the world. Sometimes just getting to the theatre is one more life skill to be learned.

Another Detour reality is that I must consider which actors cannot be put together. There are certain actors that feed off of each other. What is typical behavior to manage in other companies is magnified in our world.

I also need to look at which actors are unable to move or are less predictable. I can't put a big, strong guy right next to a girl who's more frail. There are times when they've been dancing that I've been concerned about arms being twisted off.

If four boys are moving together, it's usually much better if they're all about the same size. That way they don't step on and smash each other quite as often. Many of my actors are not steady on their feet and safety is a huge consideration. I watch for problems with balance constantly. This affects casting—The actor who played Cogsworth in *Beauty and the Beast* couldn't manage to walk up a step. I truly wanted to cast him in the role so I knew I had to change both my set design and the blocking.

One additional tip, make sure you are going to love working with every actor that requires additional help. You're about to fill every empty space in an already full schedule. This dedicated practice time requires follow through. You need to love the teaching-directing relationship or there will be burn out and frustration.

Double casting

Because of the size of our group we have begun double casting our shows. There are just too many talented men and women who audition and who can handle a role with lines and even solo songs. I needed to give more actors an opportunity and this has become a win-win solution in many ways. I double cast more than just the leading roles. By double casting all of the speaking parts, our previously shy actors who began with only one line on stage, are now able to play larger supporting roles. Double cast actors work with their "double" studying their lines together. They watch each other during rehearsals offering encouragement and feed back to each other while helping out when things become difficult. Each actor then plays their speaking part in two performances. When they are not playing that character, they become part of the chorus, making that group even stronger with their presence. This means our double cast actors are on stage for all four performances; gaining two entirely different perspectives of the show.

The coaches who work with the double cast actors and perform with them during the production face very unique challenges. In *Beauty and the Beast*, for example, the beast's coach worked with one actor who has Down Syndrome and another actor who is on the Autism spectrum. Each performer had a different set of performance skills. While blocking was basically the same, each actor had their own unique perspective.

Announcing their parts

Announcing the cast to the actors is very hard and always, ALWAYS emotional. I usually begin with a pledge:

> I am not going to complain, (I am not going to complain)
> If my role is huge, (repeat)
> Or not so huge
> I am going to make my role spectacular
> I am not going to count my lines
> I'm not going to compare my role to anyone elses'
> And if I have a problem
> I will not cry
> No matter what
> I will do my best
> And love everyone in this room
> I know that I am part of making this show
> Spectacular and magical
> The end

A shorter pledge is:

> If my part is big or little (repeat)
> My job is to

Have fun
Support the show
And be magical

These pledges change as needed. For example:

Put your hand over your heart and repeat:
I know (repeat)
I am really essential
I am really beautiful
And I am really important to this show
And I'm going to dance my heart out
And I am not going to count how many lines I have.

I have announced their parts in different ways. Sometimes I hang huge posters with the cast and assignments on the wall and let them look at the parts they have. I am prepared for tears as well as elation.

If I feel like the process is going to be especially hard on someone or if I know many are not going to get the parts they want, I will talk to them about the process first. Then I will announce the roles, starting with the chorus first, the lead characters last. One of the more successful ways to assign parts is to begin by pairing the actors with their show coaches.

I tell the actors that if they do not understand the importance of their role, they just haven't seen the full picture yet. Every actor in the room is absolutely essential, much to the nightmare of the costumers. By the show weekend everyone has the chance to develop a wonderful role.

Every time we cast a play I remind the group that not everybody may get the role they want. We have to share. If they were a lead in the last play, then it's time to give someone else that chance. I remind them that we have to cast our version of "age appropriate." For example, when casting both *Hairspray* and *Footloose,* we needed a large group of high school students. I had to tell the actors who were over 40 that it's really hard to make them look like teenagers. They had to accept being cast as adults.

Finally, I remind each of my actors to learn something from each production. It doesn't matter how big your role is. It does matter how big your performance is, how you perform it and that you infuse it with heart.

CHAPTER 8

Becoming Characters

After casting a show, in those very beginning show rehearsals, the coaches and I spend a great deal of time working on helping actors to explore exactly who their character is and how he or she fits into the story. I begin with an exercise where the actors, sitting in small groups with their coaches, fill out a simple but important questionnaire. I tell them that their job is to first answer questions that will help them get to know themselves. Once that's finished, they have to answer these same questions about their characters. Recognizing similarities and differences is really important. These questions can be responded to either verbally or in writing. These questions vary but all reflect elements of: What do you like to do best? What are you most scared of? How old are you? What's your living situation? Who is your sweetheart, your best friend? I go on to ask them to describe themselves in three words—smart, pretty, 25—bold, handsome, loner etc. Finally, with my last question, I want to really engage their imagination. I invite them to tell me something I may not know about them—I'm really allergic to cats, I hate strawberries. On the other side of the paper (or in discussion) I ask them to answer the very same questions about their character. Who is your character? What's your character's name?

How old is your character in this story? We repeat the list question for question.

I explain to my actors that we do this because they don't want to be in a play acting as themselves. The fun of being in a play is acting out somebody else's life and situation. As an actor you want to explore other characters. That's the goal. It's why we should leave our troubles at the door. It's why we dare to do something we may not normally do. When we are on stage we are someone other than who we are in real life. When we are on stage it's all about that journey of discovery.

After working on character descriptions we often add another exercise. I tell them they are going to get up and go meet the other people who live in the village or town where the play takes place. I tell them to move around the room, walk and introduce themselves—in character. They have a chance to really question the group and ask, "Who are you?" "How do you fit in here?" I send them off with a, "On your mark, get set, go." And off they go mingling and beginning to understand who their character is and how their character relates to the others of that community. This is a grand learning process for who they will later become on stage.

A final rule I try to maintain is that when they're on stage—our actual stage or practice space—they are to refer to one another by character names. This helps with a lot of things. It encourages us to stay in the story. It takes away the sting when they forget to do something or if something needs to be corrected. I remind them— "That character must remember to enter"—or "that character would never behave in that way." Best of all if there's a slip up on stage, actors don't stop mid-sentence and say, "No Christopher "— he's not Christopher, he's Lurch and if Lurch needs to move that's how to address him. (This is a real help, not only for the actors, but for the coaches who may need this reminder tool)

CHAPTER 9

Coaches

Coaches are the "glue" of every Detour show and of every Detour practice. Without them we couldn't do the complex work we do. Our coaches come from all over. Some are theater students, others are teachers, retired business people, caregivers. We even use a few parents—parents who truly care and are able to help with someone other than their own son or daughter.

If I had to write a job description for *a* coach it would be this: You must love theater so much that the passion for creating theater is bigger than your passion for free time or money. The other thing you must have is a heart so enormous that you can give to your actor (s) without any expectation of what you will get back. Every coach is a gift—they share time, encouragement, learning strategies, and the belief needed to make their actor(s) succeed. The reward is huge—but so is their investment of time, heart and caring.

The exact job requirement for each of our coaches is slightly different. While the heart and passion are the same for all, the approach and follow through must be tailored to fit each unique situation. In addition to "coaching" a show, some coaches must pair their work with special skills such as pushing a wheel chair, helping to navigate a power chair, audio describing for an actor who is blind, or by providing ASL for actors who are deaf. Some situations require that a coach physically move with their actor in a hand over a hand kind of a relationship. (Just as a note, coaches do not tug, or impose movement that does not look natural or possible for an actor. We honor each individual for what movement is possible and do not want our actors to ever feel like puppets.) Creating uniformity is not the challenge for our coaches. Finding how to enhance, challenge, and inspire an actor to grow is. Always the underlying goal is to honor, celebrate and respect each actor's dignity and effort.

We experience as many unique situations as we have actors. Keeping them safe is a huge—but not always simple—goal. My son often requires a one-to-one because his behavior can be erratic. He carries an additional diagnosis of IETD—intermittent explosive temper disorder. If there is someone who knows how to hold him and talk to him, an outburst passes as quickly as it comes on. We have other actors who get lost in bathrooms. We had one very independent actor walk through a window. Coaches must be aware of their actors off-stage habits and personal tendencies as well as of their on-stage behavior related to lines and blocking.

Coaches use a combination of side coaching—(encouraging their actors from outside the role) and coaching in role (acting as Belle's best friend and in that role moving together through songs, etc.) Most often coaches use a combination of both in the same show. Knowing how much and how little support to give an actor is a real skill that grows and develops with each show they do.

> *Examples:* When we did *Fiddler* Christopher's coach, costumed just like Christopher, stood off to the side actually pantomiming the fiddling so that Christopher would know exactly what to do and when to do it. They worked as a team.

In *Hairspray* Tracy's coach acted as a friend. After Tracy made her way through the town scenes, her coach would disappear into the chorus of singers and then reappear to help as needed. Tracy's coach never got bigger than her actor. This actor had a great deal to memorize both in terms of lines and blocking, her coach was a necessary part of helping her manage all of that.

I have a few coaches who really "get" their actor and his or her learning style. They choose to stay with the same actor show after show. They develop very strong bonds of loyalty. There are other coaches who really enjoy the challenge of changing actors. It's a fluid thing. My job is to watch and listen—to see what's working and what isn't—for both groups. I tell my coaches again and again that as the glue for this work, everything sticks to them. New coaches and coaches who can't commit to coming to every rehearsal are not assigned to an individual but work as part of a coaching duo or fill in for coaches who are absent. When my actors arrive the first thing they do is to look for their sweet hearts (if they have one) but that next most important look about the room is to find their coach. If their coach isn't there, it matters and I need to have a backup plan.

Coaches help actors become comfortable both with the sequence of the story and with how their character fits. I continually remind my coaches that their most sacred job is to find those moments in the story that will make their actors feel like a "star." The challenge in a cast of 50 is that each actor wants to be (and should be) showcased. That challenge becomes an invitation to every coach to get creative. They take that challenge seriously and come up with ideas I may not have seen and can't wait to try.

Along with their actors, coaches also carry the heartbeat of the story. It's easy for our actors to get lost. Sometimes during practices I just get ahead of myself. Coaches pull me back on track. If coaches don't know what's next, I can't expect my actors to.

At rehearsals I divide the actors into the groups they will be in during the performance. I tend to use these groupings for a lot of reasons. Fifty moving actors is pure chaos. Four large moving masses of people just feels more manageable. During *Shrek,* I had the Duloc folks together, the storybook characters together, the Dragon "group" and then a final group of Shrek and Donkey. They became familiar with their scripts, their movement, the point of view and quirks of their particular group. It gives the coaches necessary support, too. They learn from one another and just as the actors show support for one another, our coaches do the same.

Because our group has grown so much, we have added a new group of coaches we call "show coaches." They get scripts and music like everyone else in the group, they get all my weekly directing notes etc. I even cast and pair them with their actors when I determine the cast at the beginning of the show. The difference is this group joins us for the rehearsals the last month before the show goes up. They are experienced coaches and they know how I work. They may have a small group or they may be used in a one-on-one situation. It depends on what is needed. They fill in where I need a last minute pair of hands to help make an actor feel comfortable and / or ensure more success in performance. They are an additional and essential support at just the moment I need it most.

I regularly schedule "coach only" run throughs with my coaches to review their entrances, their exits, and, most important, why they're making them. I stress over and over that when they're exiting the stage, they aren't just exiting, they're leaving for a reason—one they need to know from the script or one they make up and can convey to their actor. As they leave, they need to be aware of when and why they come on the stage again. There is never an exit that's not tied to an entrance. It's an essential part of blocking and they need to help their actors understand this whole process. For example, in *Shrek,* the story book characters go marching off stage because they have just been evicted from Duloc. As they leave they need to understand when and why they'll be back.

Many of the coaches aren't necessarily familiar with all the information theatre folks take for granted. They learn right along with their actors. What's really fun is watching how the actors help teach the coaches how to coach them. Now many of our actors will tell their coaches exactly where they are supposed to stand, and precisely what they need for support.

There are times that I have to remind my coaches that it's not their show, that it's the actors' show. There's a huge temptation to out dance, out act their actor or at least be just as big. When that happens, the audience has a hard time knowing who they're to watch. It's hard to tell a fabulous coach to blend—but if they're doing it right, that's exactly what must happen.

Early on in the process we act out that really important situation. I tell my actors, "Actors, if you don't want your coaches to be bigger than you, what must you do?" There's always lots of laughter. "Don't let anyone steal your moment." I caution them. "If you don't want your coach to be bigger than you, then you must be bigger." I don't care if my actors have a million lines or if they have two—I want them to shine and, most of all, I want them to feel proud.

CHAPTER 10

Choreography

My actors love to dance. They love to create movement that's free, uncensored and theirs. Their dance comes from the heart. I tell them to dance with abandon, even those with limited physical ability. At the same time they all have to manage the basics of real choreography. Every dance is a combination of both pure heart and planned movement.

Teaching choreography to our actors is very different. When I tell them to copy or learn a dance, many of them get lost or frustrated in what their bodies can't quite manage or do. The goal for me is to find a way—through a great deal of careful watching and a lot of breaking down of steps—for their bodies to inhabit my planned movement until the movement becomes more natural, makes sense and becomes theirs. The way most people learn movement, is to first see it with their eyes which in turns signals the brain, which then sends messages to the correct body parts to respond. In any part of that instantaneous message process, my actors can experience a glitch, a break down or a short circuit. We learn movement in "our" way. Our movement patterns travel from extremities (feet, hands, heads) through bodies (including hearts) and then up into our brains. Once we feel it and make the necessary connections again, again, and again, something happens—you see it. There's always that vital connection "through the heart." That's where they feel and get the motivation to stick with it until learning really happens.

For most people, as you move the lower part of your body you naturally take your pelvis with you. You also swing your arms without thinking in opposition to your feet. That's tricky for many of our actors. For some it's crossing the mid line that pushes them off balance. For others, it's moving the arms in one way while moving the legs in the opposite way that creates a challenge. Still others just need an additional step added to a sequence in order to regain their footing. We need to solve each of these situations. It all seems impossible, but together we figure it out.

There is one basic rule for choreography with this group, "simplify." It can't be said enough. Simplify patterns of movement. Simplify focus. Simplify the amount of steps. Simplify how we turn. Simplify how we connect to others. After all the simplifying there's still the invitation to dance, and they do. When we had auditions for *Fiddler,* we taught the traditional grape vine step. Only a few could actually execute the complexities of that pattern but we still chose to teach that because we wanted them to stretch. From there we began to back off and figure out what would really work for us. Both with the movement of the feet and the linking of arms we needed to simplify. We added an extra chorus of music so no one felt hurried. They had to get it in little pieces. Our grapevine morphed into a step-together-step-together pattern. Everyone ended up with their own variation of raised arms. I'm sure the community of Anatevkah had to make similar adjustments. They carried the power of the dance without the complexity. It worked.

With every show there's a dance challenge. It may be a box step, a pivot turn, a waltz, or even a tango. We practice slowly, very slowly. We work hand over hand. We work with my dancing behind one actor as another coach dances behind their partner. We work with mirroring. We work with counting and moving our arms before we add in our legs. With some that miracle of getting it starts to happen. They begin to play with taking that step across the midline, or box step, pivot or whatever a dance requires. They make it their own and in that four months of practice they are able to succeed. For others the miracle is in finding the right adjustment. Either way we cheer.

It is difficult to bring in outside choreographers. We can ask for ideas and look for fun movement but we can't, with any big success, "pre plan" in the way most choreographers like to work. We don't over choreograph on paper. We see what works on bodies, individual bodies. Everyone has their different abilities and needs. The trick, and ultimate success, is in finding the individual movements an actor can do and weaving those into a cohesive dance. Drawing from what I see them do on their own is best. That means I watch both their movement and the way they tweak, change, adjust, and follow through with mine. It allows me to celebrate what they contribute to the whole and it gives everyone a sense of ownership.

With choreography, I definitely always have something in mind. But I have to put it on their bodies first. If it doesn't fit, I alter it. The biggest challenge to this process is me. I have to be willing to let go of the moment I have pre-choreographed. I can be sure my stuff looks really great, but I always need to remind myself to step back and look. If it doesn't work I must be willing to throw it out and try a different approach.

Dance is where individuality is celebrated first and always. When we are ready to perform before an audience, I don't care if it all doesn't look the same. I want it to look like US—us, at our very, very best. There is no place in this work for competition, discouragement or comparison.

CHAPTER 11

Learning Lines

While it is true that memorizing lines isn't as huge a challenge to some, it is still definitely one of the greatest challenges faced by the vast majority of our actors. For most, repetition is the key. That, paired with kinesthetic cues, seems to help immensely. The actors who are usually most successful are the ones who also have help from home. I work with the principal actors on their lines at special rehearsals—usually weekly. This is a great time to take lines apart and really talk about their meaning. Running and reviewing again and again seems to be the key to learning BUT equally important is the complete understanding of the meaning, timing and significance of what they have to say.

During rehearsals I ask my coaches to run their actors' lines any time there is a pause in the process. Coaches need to know these lyrics and lines as well their actors, maybe even better. It's also a part of that coach's responsibility to know how and when to cue their actors to say those lines. Sometimes "cueing" means giving the first word of a line. Other times it means quietly whispering a full sentence. Sometimes it means getting the show back on track when lines have been cut or improvised. I'm always there to cue actors from in front of the stage—including during our performances. I sit with an open script as a safe guard. If a line gets missed, or a lyric is forgotten I chime in. The audience doesn't really even notice my voice and is truly all-forgiving. Memorization is not nearly as important to us as teaching the how and why of that line's delivery.

There are other important issues related to learning lines. Some actors just need to learn how to slow down. Others need help with pronunciation. I will often ask "What's the most important letter in any word you say?" For us, the answer is the final consonant. Example, " I want to go out." Going for that final "t" really helps both with clarity and forcing them to slow down their delivery. This lesson is hugely valuable for us. When you finish a word it helps the audience to really understand it. For those who can, we put this skill to good use. For those who can't, it's simply a goal. Many of our actors have true pronunciation challenges. If an actor tries to say something again and again without success, we simply change the word. The process we teach is about facilitating possibility not incurring frustration. Sometimes the best magic is in finding just the right word that CAN be said.

I often work with actors individually to teach them how to make the right sound. I watch closely. I try to figure out for myself why a word gets stuck. Does it have to do with the brain? Is it related to how the tongue moves? Is it about memory? This time spent with an actor can't be hurried. It's where real "detours" happen in the teaching process.

Many of my actors have very minimal speech and when they get stressed, (and that can be either the good stress of excitement or the bad stress of great pressure on them) the words just get stuck somewhere within their brain. In order for a word to be pronounced a message need to pass from dendrite to dendrite. It seems that sometimes those dendrites curl up and that the message falls in a cavity in between. It's not that an actor can't say a certain word, it's just that at that specific moment in time the message can't successfully get through to the part of the brain that allows articulation to happen.

One of the most important rehearsal deadlines for me as a director is the rehearsal when all must be "off book." That means no scripts on stage. That's the day real movement and interaction begins. That's the day they begin looking at one another. And most of all that's the day I figure out who's really memorized their part. "Off book" forces memorization. It's that nudge and deadline that says, "get to work now if you want to really act." Usually I set that "off book" date at least two weeks before I actually MUST have it happen.

Not all the actors can remember all their lines, even those cast in leading roles. That's okay. The actress I cast as Tracy in *Hairspray* had a huge amount of material to memorize. More important to me was that she embodied the heart of Tracy. I told her, "You can miss a line, and all you have to do is wriggle your hips and they won't care. Show that smile, you are Tracy." The audience loved her performance. They knew nothing of her missed lines and any I noticed I forgot about immediately.

I end many a rehearsal saying "Know that I love you. Learn your lines. Have fun. Learn your lines!"

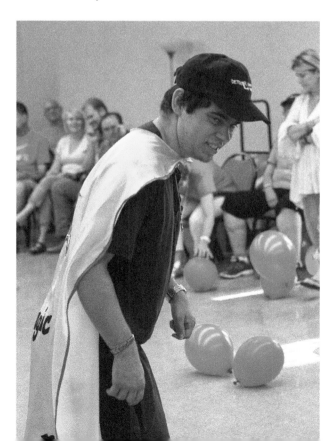

CHAPTER 12

Music

Music is the Velcro of everything we do. We teach volumes of skills through music. Everything sticks to it—it's flexible, it's strong, and it's incredibly magical. I have found musical theater is the best vehicle in the world to contain these wonderful hearts and spirited voices. It is a vehicle—it keeps moving us forward. Over the years we have grown in our musical ability, just as we have grown in our acting. Because of that, we are now tackling musicals we would never have believed possible when we began.

Personally, as a director/choreographer, choosing and then working with a musical director I can trust is essential. I depend on and value their knowledge to guide the musical direction of the show. In our very first years we began by using cassettes (yes, Detour is that old.) Very quickly I figured out we needed to use live music. I also figured out that we not only needed someone who knew music but someone who was willing to know and understand the ability and needs of our actors.

Our director of music has to detourize music in much the same way I detourize a script. He patiently teaches the actors the music. Detour is not Detour without a loud chorus belting out songs.

We begin our rehearsal process by teaching lyrics. There are two reasons for this. First, many of our actors have watched the movies of most of the plays we do so they are familiar with the songs. We need to help those who aren't familiar catch up. Second, as soon as possible, we want to give each of our actors a rehearsal CD of our show music. It saves a great deal of time and frustration to learn the music first so our "show music" CD reflects more accurately what we expect the actors to learn. With a show our actors don't know at all, the teaching time is much greater.

Singing is a different kind of learning—it comes from the other side of the brain. It's all about the melody, rhythm and a right brain celebration. Often the words happen in rhyme—at the very least they have a pattern. Especially for my actors who stammer, when I ask them to sing a message all of a sudden they have vocal fluency. They're engaging a whole different set of responses. For those reasons music, singing the songs, is pure joy and communicates everything.

After a few sit down sessions where they learn the words to a song, we get up and move. We learn a kick or a gesture for specific words and we begin learning the choreography as we sing.

Detour has had two musical directors. Our first began by accompanying 4 songs. Then we transitioned to his underscoring dialogue and playing during transitions. Slowly we began adding other musicians during productions. This "show band" has become essential. Detour's production values steadily increased as I chose shows to keep up with this truly talented musician. We now regularly use three to four other musicians along with our musical director who is at the piano and/or keyboard conducting. My musical director is an essential part of every step in the process and a valued partner.

When our first musical director left we were blessed to bring on our current, equally inspiring, "magician" of music. Like Stephen, David can do anything at a keyboard - and does. I encourage each of these artists to write a book on their own "Detour Process." I can't fully comprehend or describe the "how" of everything they do to teach, conduct, and accompany us. I only know music, resounding music, is what fuels the group every practice. It fills our hearts and inspires us to keep doing the work we do.

CHAPTER 13

Adapting Sets

We strive to give our mainstage shows full production value. We perform in a real theater. Our desire is to give our actors and our audiences an authentic theater experience. Along with flats and platforms, we use Detour designed wooden boxes for sitting, for creating tables, beds and a host of other things in every show. We have step units of varying heights and a ramp. Everything is created according to the needs of our group.

Where Detour differs from the average theater company is with the very real challenge of making all these steps, platforms and other pieces accessible to our actors and their specific needs. Our set designer is about safety first. Safety has to do with not slipping. The top surfaces of platforms should be painted with no skid paint. We're very careful about what kind of a rake there is on a platform or ramp and what kind of a rise there is on a step. We have to make sure that a platform can hold ample bodies. We can't have narrow steps. We have found ours need to be wider than normal steps because many of our actors are more dominate on one side. They step-together-step-together rather than alternating legs as they walk. Creating wider stairs honors that need.

Sometimes we use a ramp instead of stairs so that we can accommodate an actors mobility issues. A ramp gives opportunity to a group of actors who otherwise couldn't do a particular scene. That doesn't mean a ramp serves only those using wheel chairs. In *Beauty and the Beast,* it was much easier for several of our actors to move up a ramp rather than use steps. We choose to do what's most successful AND what's most comfortable. Ramps do take up more space—they're worth it—just take that into consideration for set planning.

Dick, our "director of sawdust creations," carefully plans for this group. He rounds the corners of our boxes and steps for saftey. He makes everything as light as possible so that actors can carry various items to new positions as needed.

The sooner you can get your set pieces into your rehearsal space the better. Changes and adaptations to the set almost always have to happen. The set designer is another essential part of the team and needs this time to work out solutions.

We host set painting days where we invite actors, families and other volunteers. This day not only prepares the set but provides a fun bonding experience for everyone.

CHAPTER 14

Importance of Props

Everyone loves working with props. They make a scene real. We have had lots of fun with magical machines, fireplaces, and a beanstalk that grew. Props become a show saver for me and for many of our more challenged actors. My son has trouble attending for any length of time in a group. During *"Hairspray"* he was having a difficult time paying attention. We decided that we would cast him as the TV camera operator in the big dance scene. Our set designer created a stand up, true to life looking, camera from a card board box. He equipped it with a battery and a switch that clicked on and off with a flashing red light on top. Christopher went from having a role where he did nothing and was bored to a role where he said "5,4,3,2,1—roll em." He clicked on the red light and was thrilled. A prop, that camera, gave him his moment to shine.

Props help us out in other ways. Often props become a tool to help relieve the anxiety that leads to other more self-destructive behavior. Some of our actors play with their fingers. Others bite or scratch themselves when they become nervous or stressed or bored. These behaviors are distracting for everyone when they are doing them during a rehearsal and even worse, they are disturbing for audience members during a show. Our challenge is to find props or costume pieces that address these behaviors. We may ask an actor to hold on to and push a wheelchair with a coach, to carry a parasol, or even to wear appropriate looking gloves. It's a matter of creating "show tools" to keep them honestly engaged and focused on the task at hand.

Actors carrying objects can also be very charming. Ed always arrived with his own personal prop, Cupcake, a little, scruffy stuffed toy puppy that he held in his hand or who rode in his pocket. When Ed danced he danced with Cupcake and he moved him around when he talked. The costumers loved Cupcake, making miniature costumes for him to match what Ed was wearing for many a show. Actors, coaches and audiences all loved Cupcake and he became part of our company.

It doesn't matter if it's a 20 ft. dragon or the "machine that saved the world." Props are what help the audience see the story and motivate the actors. They're not only fun, but they may become just the thing needed to bring out an actor's special moment to shine. In *The Addams Family* our set designer created a "Torture Chair." As Lurch lowered a bar on one side of the chair, lights went on and there was an electrical sound effect. Our Lurch had the best time "torturing" whoever sat in the chair. To truly offer an authentic theatre experience, props are an essential, engaging part of the magic.

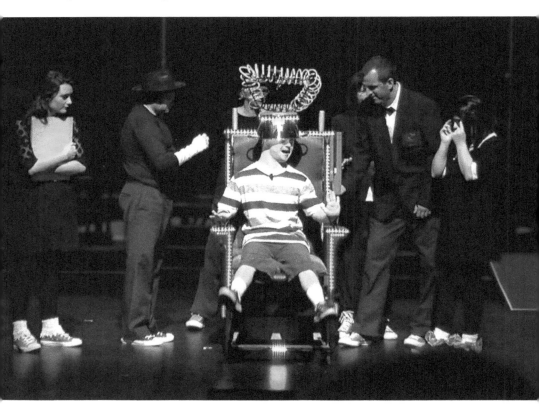

CHAPTER 15

Costumes

Costumes make the character. Actor's feel special the moment they slip on a costume piece. It makes their character come to life—for them and for the audience. We endeavor to costume everyone, including the coaches. The goal is to make each character as beautiful, scary, or as magical as he or she should be. In *"Beauty and the Beast,"* an actor who struggles with vocal fluency was cast as keeper of the rose. We knew that if she felt beautiful she would be truly dazzling and confident. Our goal was to make her look truly magical so she embodied the spirit of the rose. In the production she beamed as she dropped her flower petals.

We have a few Detour considerations for our costuming. We put all of our actors in Converse shoes because they have flat soled bottoms that add to our actors' stability as they walk and dance. With everyone in Converse shoes everyone's feet look unique yet similar. Though some of our actors could wear character shoes, many can't because they have balance problems. Converse shoes are a unifying element. At the same time actors are encouraged to choose their own color and style which then celebrates their individuality.

© 2018 Christine Keith

We can and do change the look of our shoes. We added striped socks for *Seussical*. We painted a pair gold for Cinderella. For *Footloose*, a gifted costumer made twenty pair of spats that went over the top of the Converse to transform them into cowboy boots.

Our actors are adult men and women who are very interested in other men and women. Because many actors have mobility problems, it's very hard for them to scurry down stairs to change costumes. We make our costume changes back stage. Because it may be awkward to ask an actor to whip off their shirt or drop a skirt, we put the girls in a base costume which consists of some kind of a legging or a short biker short with a camisole top or a sports bra with a tank top over it. On top of that they can put on their show costumes, shirts, dresses and cummerbunds, etc. In *Beauty and the Beast,* many of the village people had a quick change in order to become silverware. All they had to do was let their skirts drop, take off their blouses and slip on their aprons which transformed them into knives, forks and spoons.

We use Velcro on almost every costume to aid in fast changes. Velcro also helps us reuse costumes. Velcro waste bands allow us to accommodate ever changing sizes.

Makeup and hair are another important part of helping create character. Most of the actors love getting this done before the performance. We have volunteers who do make up and we have a professional salon stylist come in to do hair. She shapes and designs hair to fit each actor's character. She made bee hives for *Hairspray,* duck tails for *Grease* and everything in between.

Because this group of actors has trouble keeping track of all their costume pieces we put together a bag for each. Inside is every costume piece that doesn't require a hanger. On the outside of the bag is the actors name and a checklist of every item that belongs inside. We always tell the actors everything you take off goes into your bag. That way, because we do more than one performance, everything is kept together. In our most recent production we had over 500 different costume parts for 50 actors and 20 coaches. The bags kept us responsible, organized and sane.

CHAPTER 16

Post Show "Hot Seat" Celebration

After four months of working together, ending a show is difficult for everyone. We all experience sadness mixed with a tiny bit of relief, as well as genuine pride in accomplishing what often feels impossible. It's hard for actors to let go of a show. To help us deal with this profound mixture of feelings, we have an important ritual the week after the show ends. It's called a Hot Seat party. The Hot Seat celebration gives the actors something to look forward to after that final curtain comes down. It allows all of us to decompress, and we get to talk about our feelings. It's all about that important moment of evaluation and reflection.

Sitting in chairs in our large circle, I begin by asking the actors how they felt about the show just finished. They tell the group what their parents, friends, or relatives have told them. It's a nice beginning to our get together. Then we get into the real purpose of the time together, the Hot Seat.

The Hot Seat goes like this. There is a lone chair in the center of our circle. I start by telling everyone the rules, the most important being only positive comments are to be shared. One at a time, each actor walks to the Hot Seat, proudly, because it's their moment to be congratulated. They sit down, then choose three people who will say something about what they did on stage. One of the three people they choose must be their coach. The other two people can be anyone whose arm is waving in the air. After three comments, the actor takes a final bow and we give them one big clap.

The comments people make to each other are always supportive and often surprising. "You were wonderful. " I'm so proud of the way you danced, you sang, you learned your lines." We have never had a problem with negative comments. The Hot Seat has become a wonderful way for all of us to celebrate the end of a magical performance.

At the end, we Hot Seat the coaches and designers. They stand in a large circle with their backs to one another facing out to the group. The actors have an opportunity to move all around this circle thanking and talking to each of the coaches who have been there to support them. Doing the coaches circle this way is a time saver and an equalizer. It gives actors the opportunity to make more personal comments, and ALL the coaches feel celebrated— even those whose actors may not have the words or ability to say thanks.

One note for the Hot Seat, if it's possible, you can use your favorite "sit upon" set piece. *The Addams Family* torture chair has been the favorite so far.

Conclusion

I'm often asked what makes Detour, Detour. When you ask the actors, one of the first things they say is, "welcoming." This is closely followed by a series of comments that can all be lumped together under the word "family." I would have to agree—both welcoming and family do define us, but the definition of Detour is broader than that. We are like an aquarium full of uniquely quirky and absolutely dazzling fish. What makes this aquarium so special is the fact that it's filled with these captivating differences. That is the truth of Detour's family. We began as an organization "for those with cognitive challenges," but we have grown far beyond that. As I was driving one of my actors home one day, we talked about the wording on the Detour t-shirt she wore so proudly. It was our first year and I had struggled with finding just the right wording that would define us. Her shirt, one of our first, read "making a journey in the arts possible for those with cognitive challenges. I asked her (always best to ask the actors—Detour is their organization.) She looked at me and said, "We're much more than that. We're everyone who wants a chance." I took her words to heart. That show we changed our logo to read "... making a journey in the arts possible for all."

Two important things worth noting. It IS challenging to work with all these different groups. It means we need more coaches and it means we have to either find or train coaches in specific skill sets that an actor requires. Both of those are doable. It means we need to really get to know our actors on a deeply individual basis. Each actor requires something different.

The other note—and I share it humbly—is that I have discovered that no matter how much I want to be, we are not realistically there "for all." I do realize there are those that we can't heal, control, or somehow make life better for. There are others who do NOT want this experience no matter how much their parents want it for them. There are some who simply cannot handle the stimulation of a room full of 50-60 moving bodies. We hope the "beginning" group works for them but sometimes even that may be too much chaos. There are some who come to find sweethearts, others who are overly aggressive. In either of these cases I say, "No." We are social but not a dating service. Finally, we are not equipped to handle profound psychological issues that may prove to be dangerous for others.

We are richer and better for making a commitment to inclusiveness and diversity. We have actors who come as they are, living with whatever condition they have. We don't ask many questions about that "condition." We ask about their dreams and why they want to act. We adjust and do what we need to do to ensure success. We learn to count steps and we understand what it means to watch where we're going. We understand that getting a script Brailled is only the first step. We sign and if we can't sign we learn the value of gestures, facial expression and simply giving focus to an actor who is Deaf. We learn what it is that an individual needs whether they live with Autism, Down Syndrome, Angelman's Syndrome or a host of other "stuff." We do not teach to a disability. We teach to an actor. Within each of them, we recognize there is a deep down desire to act, to be celebrated, to be part of a community– a brilliantly unique fish in this tremendously huge tank full of diverse humanity.

We love the slice of life we present. No matter how different we each are, we have this one great shared dream. It's the acceptance we experience and the celebration of our uniqueness that makes us family. It's our commitment to authentic practice that makes us a theatre company.

Recently, our logo took one more "Detour." Now it says simply, Theatre Together. For us, that says it all.

Epilogue

Our world is calling us to be more . . . both as individuals and as a theatre company. As I was editing this book I got a text from an actor. In her sweet way, she summed up everything we're about. Two of her relatives were tragically killed in the horrific carnage of the Pittsburgh Temple shooting. Her text to me asked only one thing. "When I get to Detour Thursday can I have a huge Detour hug?" I answered "absolutely" without thinking twice. Then I stopped and thought about that request. I need to explain these Detour hugs . . . there are times in our lives when we really need to experience the support of a truly caring community. So there are times we place an actor in the center of the room and just "glom on." Yes, we all hug that actor and each other, until we're simply a mass of humanity standing entwined—tough to tell where one of us lets off and another of us begins. This interwoven mass is Detour at its best. I've come to realize it's what I want Detour to stand for in this world. I want us to look like an interwoven, connected mass of humanity who believes huge good is possible, that is there for one another, and that, in the end, continues because of the stories of kindness, acceptance, and daring we tell. In this mass of arms and friendship we don't notice politics, religion, color, quirks, and/ or sexual orientation . . . we take in the warmth, the bonds, the strength of one another—just as we are. May we brilliantly share our differences—yes —but, when it is all said and done, Detour exists because we see only a family — shared dreams, shared daring, shared determination.

CPSIA information can be obtained
at www.ICGtesting.com
Printed in the USA
JSHW021644271219
3194JS00002B/1